Did Saint Augustine of Hippo ever own a Hippopotamus?

THUY VU

Did Saint Augustine Ever Own A Hippopotamus?
Text and Illustration Copyright: by Thuy Vu
Published: March 2014

ISBN-13: 978-1502559739
ISBN-10: 1502559730

All rights reserved. No part of this publication may be reproduced, stored in a retrieval system, or transmitted in any form or by any means – electronic, mechanical, photocopy, recording, or any other – except for brief quotations in printed reviews, without the prior permission of the author.
You must not circulate this book in any format.

Who was Saint Augustine of Hippo?

What a strange name!

Did he have a hippopotamus?

Saint Augustine of Hippo was born in 354 CE in an ancient north African city called Thegaste.

Yes, like Augustine, hippos also live in Africa! But that is not how he got his title.

Read on, and you will see.

When Augustine was young, his mother Monica would wake up very early, before the sun came up. Why? To pray for her little boy as he slept.

Rather than asking God to give Augustine gold and fame, she asked that he would treasure God.

Although his mother kept praying for him, Augustine spent his free time with friends who liked to bully and laugh at people. They called themselves "The Wreckers."

Do you think that you would want friends like Augustine's?

Probably not.

Augustine did a lot of things that made his mother sad. Once, he took pears from an orchard just because he wanted to steal something. And he didn't even like pears!

So Augustine's mom prayed even harder for God to change his heart and make it beautiful…

and God was listening.

He was nineteen years old when he had a son named Adeodatus, meaning "gift from God".

Augustine didn't know who God was, but God already knew Augustine, and He always heard Monica's prayers for her son.

One day Augustine found a book by Cicero, called **Hortensius**. It sparked his love for asking hard questions like "What is the purpose of life?" and "Is there a God?"

For ten years, Augustine searched for answers. He believed in the religion of the Manichees. After following them for ten years, he was as lost and empty as when he started.

Augustine also searched for other ways to fill his life. He looked to money, fame, and public service.

Do you think these will make you truly happy?

Augustine worked as a teacher in Carthage, and then in Rome. When he saw that his students were as naughty as he was, he moved again to Milan.

Even though he moved from city to city, his mother always found a way to stay close to him, and she kept praying for her son.

Through his mother and a bishop named Ambrose, Augustine did learn about God. In Milan, Bishop Ambrose explained God's message:

Though Augustine lived a selfish and wicked life, God sent His Son Jesus to die in Augustine's place.

Augustine struggled still.
If Jesus took his punishment,
wouldn't he owe his whole life to God?

One day, Augustine sat on a bench.
He did not want to believe in God.
Augustine did not want to surrender
his life to God.

Far away, he heard a child's voice sing
"pick up and read, pick up and read!"
So he picked up the Bible and
read Romans chapter 13.
The words spoke to his heart.

At that moment, peace and joy filled his heart. He was changed forever.

The God of the Bible is true!
Through Jesus's death on the
cross, he had eternal life!

Smiling from ear to ear, Augustine was baptized by Bishop Ambrose. Augustine and his mom loved to talk about God together.
God answers prayers!

Afterward, Augustine wrote many books, including *The Confessions* and *The City of God*. God used him to convince men throughout the ages of God's truth and power.

But wait!
What about the hippos?

As far as we know, Augustine never had a hippo. However, after leaving Milan, he moved to an African city called Hippo Regius! Later, he became the Bishop of Hippo Regius.

Augustine took on the city's name as part of his title. He was known as Augustine of Hippo.

Like calling someone Johnny of New York, or Sally of Houston, the title helped others know where you came from.

What would your title be?

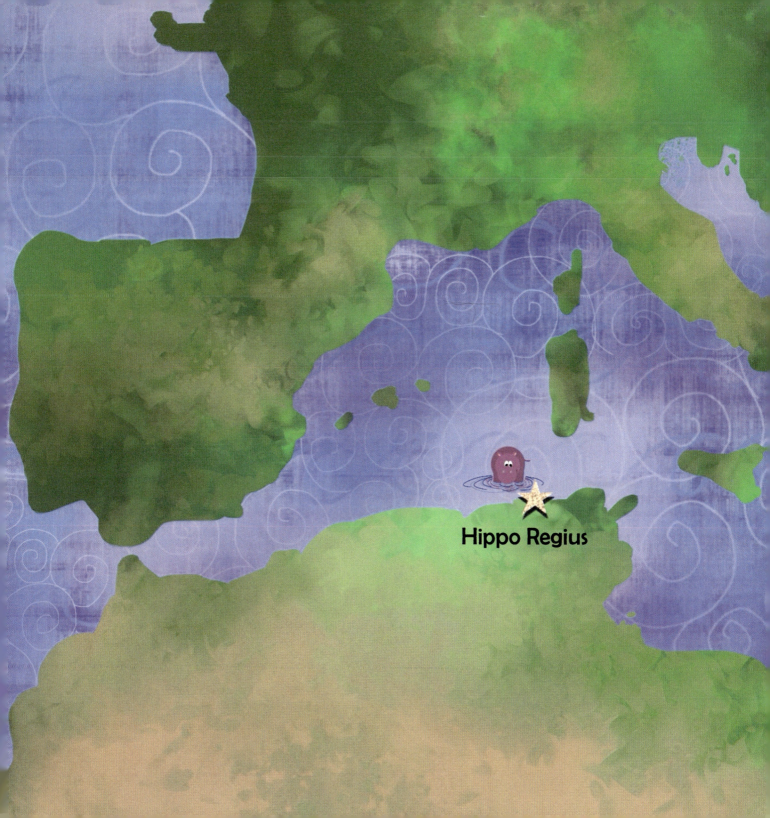

On August 28, 430 CE, Augustine passed away.

At the same time, barbarians destroyed the city of Hippo—
but Augustine's library was saved.

Because of this, we can still read Augustine's books today and hear his wonderful thoughts about God.

"Because God has made us for Himself,
we are restless until we rest in Him."

-Saint Augustine of Hippo

Made in the USA
Las Vegas, NV
11 November 2021